Kailin Gow's Go Girl Guide to Being More Productive

GUIDE for BUSY PEOPLE ON THE GO

KAILIN GOW

Kailin Gow

Kailin Gow's Go Girl Guide to Being More Productive
Published by Sparklesoup Inc.
Copyright © 2023 Kailin Gow

All Rights Reserved. No part of this book may be reproduced or transmitted in any form or by any means, graphic, electronic, or mechanical, including photocopying, recording, taping or by any information storage or retrieval system, without the permission in writing from the publisher except in case of brief quotations embodied in critical articles and reviews.

For information, please contact:

Sparklesoup Inc.
11700 W. Charleston Blvd. #170-95
Las Vegas, NV 89135
www.sparklesoup.com
First Edition.
Printed in the United States of America.

Kailin Gow's Go Girl Guide to BEING MORE PRODUCTIVE

DEDICATION

To my family and friends for encouraging me to write books I believe in. And to my fans for being the best cheerleaders, beta testers, and super fans an author can dream of. This book about being more productive is for you so you can be even more Super!

Kailin Gow

Table of Content

CHAPTER ONE 6
- THE POWER OF MORNING ROUTINES....... 6

CHAPTER TWO 18
- THE IMPORTANCE OF SETTING PRIORITIES 18

CHAPTER THREE 28
- TIME MANAGEMENT 28

CHAPTER FOUR 43
- OVERCOMING PROCRASTINATION 43

CHAPTER FIVE 53

Kailin Gow's Go Girl Guide to BEING MORE PRODUCTIVE

DEVELOPING A POSITIVE ATTITUDE 53

CHAPTER SIX **71**

    PLANNING AHEAD 71

CHAPTER SEVEN **79**

    REVIEWING YOUR PROGRESS 79

CONCLUSION **97**

Kailin Gow

Introduction

Would you like to be more productive? Most people would answer with a resounding "yes!" The good news is that being more productive is not as difficult as it may seem. Adopting some of the habits of highly productive people can significantly increase your productivity.

With ever-increasing demands on our time, it's more important than ever to make the most of every minute.

Fortunately, you can do plenty of things to boost your productivity. By incorporating some of the top habits of highly productive people, you can supercharge your productivity and get more done in less time.

This book will discuss some helpful habits of highly productive people. We will also provide tips on how you

Kailin Gow's Go Girl Guide to BEING MORE PRODUCTIVE

can implement these habits into your own life and see an increase in productivity. Let's get started!

Kailin Gow

Chapter One

The Power of Morning Routines

It's still early. You don't want to get out of bed; much alone start your day. You're exhausted. You're snuggled up in blankets and feeling great. Today's a busy day, and you're thinking about everything you need to accomplish. You feel overburdened, so you hit "SNOOZE" one more time to give yourself some breathing room.

This is a vicious cycle that many of us find ourselves in day after day. We know we need to get up and start our day, but we just can't find the motivation to do so. After all, mornings are tough!

Keeping your first waking hour as constant as possible throughout the weeks is crucial to have a more straightforward morning. The more we struggle to make decisions, the more energy we lose. It's critical to avoid "decision tiredness" at startup by sticking to a set daily routine.

A morning ritual can increase your energy, productivity, and mood. It also creates momentum, reaching the brain's peak time for cognitive functioning (late morning).

Benefits of a Morning Routine

Many people dread waking up in the morning. Some of you may be able to spring out of bed and start working right away, but most of us have trouble. There's no need for mornings to be unpleasant; all you need is a daily routine. Having a morning habit has several advantages.

Both mental and physical health improve as a result of daily routines.

1. Prepare Yourself for the Rest of the Day

The rest of your day will be influenced by how you spend the morning. If you become rushed or sluggish, expect it to stick with you. However, a morning regimen puts you on track from when you wake up and in the correct frame of mind to take on the day. When you have a plan and know what to expect, it allows your mind to relax.

The goal is not to start your day with a list of things to do that are stressful but rather to allow yourself time for activities that set the tone for the rest of the day. Some examples of calming activities include reading, journaling, meditating, practicing yoga or stretching, and eating breakfast. These can all be done within an hour and will start your day right.

2. Increase Your Productivity

With a morning routine, you begin your day on the right foot. You're working on something meaningful and productive when you open your eyes.

Kailin Gow's Go Girl Guide to BEING MORE PRODUCTIVE

To make the most of your day, keep this mentality in mind. You'll be more likely to complete tasks if you maintain this feeling throughout the day, rather than starting many and leaving halves of them unfinished. When you've completed your workday, you'll know you accomplished everything feasible and can unwind in the evening without anxiety. Highly productive people share that they all have some sort of morning routine that they stick to. This helps set the tone for the rest of the day and allows them to be more productive overall.

3. Feel in Control

When you have many responsibilities, it may feel like you're rushing from one activity to the next. The day begins to dominate rather than the other way around. A morning routine, although it might just take up a tiny fraction of your day, maybe a step toward regaining control.

It allows you to focus on what's most essential and start your day with a sense of purpose. It also eliminates the need to decide how to spend your time each morning, which can be draining. Having a plan lets you know exactly what you need to do and can go about your day without feeling overwhelmed.

4. Lower Stress

When you don't have enough time to finish all of your tasks or worry about what comes next, stress sets in. When you establish a routine, you'll always know exactly what you should be doing and what comes next. You can complete your whole regimen without taking conscious rest. Furthermore, you'll know there's enough time to accomplish everything without rushing.

When you reduce stress, both your emotional and physical health improves. It might lower your risk of developing depression, anxiety, and illnesses like high blood pressure, heart disease, and diabetes.

Kailin Gow's Go Girl Guide to BEING MORE PRODUCTIVE

5. Develop Healthy Habits

It's easy to fall back into old patterns, such as hitting the snooze button or staying in bed with your phone rather than getting up immediately. These activities are time-consuming. It's simpler to avoid bad habits and develop beneficial ones when you have a routine. Before heading to work, you might start your day with a big breakfast, exercise mindfulness, or even make time for fitness.

You may continue to practice these healthy habits after you've finished the challenge. You may very well discover that you eat healthier, exercise more frequently, or waste less time on your phone.

6. Boost Your Energy Levels

Many individuals despise mornings because their energy levels are low early in the day. A fantastic thing about a morning routine is that it may boost your energy, especially since you have no time to be lazy and devote all your time to your planned activities.

Include a high-intensity workout, meditation, or a chilly shower in your morning routine if you need any additional energy boost.

How to Start a Morning Routine

It is simple to get into a morning routine. Simply establish a quick timetable for the morning, starting with the moment you wake up. Experiment with various sequences of tasks to see what works best for you.

Examples of Winning Morning Routines of Successful People

Do you need some ideas for your daily routine? Consider incorporating some of these famous people's morning routines into your own.

1. Tony Robbins: Cold Plunge Pool

Kailin Gow's Go Girl Guide to BEING MORE PRODUCTIVE

For the day, a cold shower is excellent for boosting your energy levels. Tony Robbins goes even further: he enters a 57-degree Fahrenheit pool to undergo a "radical change in temperature." A chilly shower will have similar effects if you don't have access to a plunge pool.

2. Tim Draper: Play Basketball

Tim Draper starts his day early with a game of basketball. He claims that this provides the release of endorphins and helps him relax. He has three eggs for breakfast (for their high amounts of protein) to keep his hunger at bay and help him concentrate.

3. Muhammad Ali: Read Inspiring Content

Muhammad Ali began his day with empowering affirmations. He hypothesized that reading the same affirmations over and over might alter his viewpoints, subsequently influencing his actions and thoughts. You may do the same to get ready for success.

4. Dr. Nick Zyrowski: Meditation

Dr. Nick Zyrowski gets up before everyone else in the family and spends 30 minutes meditating. This puts him in the correct frame of mind for the day and allows him to establish objectives.

5. Elle Russ: Mindfulness

Elle Russ, one of the world's best-selling novelists, has a morning routine that she embraces wholeheartedly: she begins her mindfulness practice before even getting out of bed. She takes a few moments to stretch and be grateful for her body and health. She then decides on an objective for the day, affirming it by speaking aloud.

No doubt planning your morning is beneficial - you just need to look at the scientific evidence of a morning routine to realize this. Plus, as you've seen from the morning routines of successful people, there's no requirement for it to be complicated. You can start one right now! Create your own morning routine and implement it the next day.

Kailin Gow's Go Girl Guide to BEING MORE PRODUCTIVE

Once you've established your morning routine, it's time to move on to other aspects of your life that need attention. A potential next step may be to improve your work-life balance. We've got some excellent suggestions for you to get started.

Chapter Two

The Importance of Setting Priorities

Life is full of twists and turns. Life's difficulties mount up one after the other. For our entire lives, we must manage several tasks simultaneously. As a result of our single-mindedness in performing all those duties in such a short time, we become side-tracked. The need for prioritizing your life arises here.

This is where organizing your daily activities can aid you. Prioritizing entails selecting one activity over another based on the urgency of each. So, why should you make time for prioritizing?

The answer is pretty simple: it allows you to focus on more important things. When you have many tasks, it's easy to get overwhelmed and not know where to start. But if you take the time to sit down and figure out what's most important, you can make a plan and work on things in the order that makes the most sense.

Not only will this save you time in the long run, but it will also help you avoid stress and feel more in control of your life. So, setting priorities is a great place to start if you're looking for ways to be more productive.

There are a few different ways you can go about setting priorities. Below are three of the most popular methods:

Effective Time-Management

It can be challenging to handle when you have many things to accomplish in one day. You will undoubtedly waste much time attempting to complete each activity in an arbitrary order. As a result, prioritizing in your life is critical.

If you arrange your tasks according to their urgency, it will be much simpler for you to finish them. You'll also save much time by doing so. This is because you'll have a timetable for the day with how much time should be spent on each activity.

In this manner, you will not squander much time on a task that is not essential. As a consequence of such effective time management, you will be able to work without anxiety and make the most of your time.

More Dedication

The more you make your mind up about the things you need to improve, the easier it will be for you to do so. You won't have to worry about missing your deadline since everything will be organized ahead of time.

Make sure you allot a specific amount of time for each operation. Prioritize the ones that need your immediate attention. Furthermore, give more time to those tasks that are in most urgent need of your attention. Doing so will guarantee that you have enough time on hand.

Kailin Gow's Go Girl Guide to BEING MORE PRODUCTIVE

The system is intended to help you keep your cool while working. You'll be more dedicated to your job since you will know everything has been organized ahead of time. Nothing can go wrong now, so there's no need to worry about anything.

Increased Productivity

You'll observe that remaining calm and composed goes a long way. Being devoted and focused on your work will help you finish it faster. As a result, the task will be finished in less time than usual, less than the average amount of time required.

You may complete one activity faster and jump to the next one sooner if you complete one job quicker. The continuation of this procedure will show you that you can accomplish more things than you thought possible. As a result, your productivity will improve.

Productivity will aid you in finishing tasks ahead of schedule. As a result, you'll be able to spend more time relaxing. Isn't it true that after a long, hard day, relaxation is greatly desired?

Boosts Motivation

When you notice an increase in your productivity, you will be pleased with the ability to complete your tasks on schedule. Human nature is such that when you achieve a goal, you desire to accomplish more of the same.

This is due to your confidence in your ability to continue working and finishing tasks on time. You know the significance of prioritizing in life now. You will be inspired to do better, leading to future success.

Top Priorities In Life

I've made it clear why you should pay attention to priorities in your life up till now. But to do so, you must first understand the things that must be given priority over others. I'm going to explain a few items that should be at the top of your list of essential priorities in life.

Kailin Gow's Go Girl Guide to BEING MORE PRODUCTIVE

So, strap in; this is where we get down and dirty.

Health

The first and most important thing to consider is your health. Nothing can surpass this. And I don't just mean physical health here. I mean both physical and mental health, which are equally crucial. Physical health provides you with the energy needed to accomplish tasks, while mental health helps you have the motivation to do so.

You won't be able to accomplish anything if you are unwell. Your poor physical health will make you fatigued and lethargic. In contrast, if your mental health is damaged, you will lose the desire to finish your chores.

As a result, prioritizing your health should be at the top of your to-do list because if you are healthy, everything will fall into place. You'll be able to move ahead in life if you exercise, get enough sleep, and eat a balanced diet.

Family And Friends

Your family and friends are, without question, the next item on this list. They come at the top of the list because you take precedence over them. Why is that? Because if you are not healthy, you will be unable to please your family, friends, and relatives.

They are there for you, whatever may happen. In difficult times, you will discover your family and friends at your side. As a result, they should be on your list of priorities.

You can't expect relationships to last on their own. Furthermore, one-sided efforts are known to be insufficient regarding connections. You must apply effort and energy if you want your loved ones to be near you.

Career

You've always worked for a steady job since you can remember. Over the years, some of you have had your parents' hard-earned money financed your education.

Kailin Gow's Go Girl Guide to BEING MORE PRODUCTIVE

You've spent many sleepless nights preparing for your exams. You won't be able to do so if you don't. Choosing something else, whether more critical or not, can severely damage your job and wasted years that should have been put to good use.

Don't forget that you must have a secure financial position to live a stress-free, healthy lifestyle. You will also struggle financially if you are having difficulties at work. Furthermore, the guilt of failing in your job can devastate your mental health.

Having a career that is able to provide you with financial support and security as well as social and personal satisfaction is a goal we should want to achieve in order to lead a more productive and meaningful life.

Today, there is the ability to work more than one jobs and have more than one career. Due to technological and better personal management of time and resources, like you picking up this book and learning how to be more productive; people are doubling, tripling, and even ten-xing their productivity in life.

Later in this book, I will provide a list of resources to help you become more productive, including nature ways to be healthier. Some solutions are instant, while others may take a while longer. But however long it takes, it is in the direction of progress, which is towards your goal of having a more productive and meaningful life.

Seeking Progress

You've come this far, and I'm sure you want to achieve more in life. After all, that's why you're reading this book, right?

If you don't prioritize your goals and work towards them diligently, you will never progress in life. You must be disciplined to stick to your plans if you want to make something of yourself. Having patience combined with drive and discipline will help you achieve your goals in the

Kailin Gow's Go Girl Guide to BEING MORE PRODUCTIVE

long run. The ability to achieve it while you learn how to achieve your goals will help you keep and maintain your goals.

Remember it is the journey that helps you build your character, resilience, strength, and capability to maintain and sustain your goals when you reach them. It is also the lessons you learn in developing systems of productivity that will help you get there, as well as stay there.

Lastly, to sustain your efforts to your goals and to drive your productivity, you must identify your passions to find meaning in your work. If not, the years will pass without any sense of achievement or forward momentum.

Chapter Three

Time Management

The process of planning and controlling how much time you spend on specific activities is known as time management. Improved time management allows individuals to complete more in a shorter period, lowers stress, and helps them achieve professional success.

Have you ever wondered how some people appear to have enough time to accomplish everything on their list, even though they always rush from one activity to the next, never seeming to finish anything, only to accomplish each task almost at the same time?

It's hard to believe that some people have less work to do. It's far more probable that they're utilizing their time more effectively, which means they've developed excellent time management skills.

Kailin Gow's Go Girl Guide to BEING MORE PRODUCTIVE

Time management is the ability to use your time effectively to accomplish what you need and want to do. It's a learned skill that anyone can develop with practice.

There are many different techniques for time management, but the key is to find the ones that work best for you and then stick with them.

Managing Your Time Wisely

As you progress to a higher level of achievement, time appears to be running out. The more successful you become, the less time you have. The following material will help you better manage your time so that you may be more productive and achieve your objectives sooner. We also have some excellent time management quotes on hand to inspire you.

There are many successful skills in managing your time effectively. Time management is a process that involves setting goals, planning and executing tasks, and monitoring progress. Doing it correctly can help you get more out of each day and improve your overall productivity.

There are several different time management techniques that you can use to increase your productivity.

Strategies To Help You Manage Your Time

There are many different time management strategies that you can use to increase your productivity. However, not all of these strategies will work for everyone. You must find a time management strategy that works best for you and your lifestyle.

Below are some of the most popular time management strategies:

1. Get Up Early

One of the best ways to increase your productivity is to get up early. You will have more time to get things done by getting up early.

Kailin Gow's Go Girl Guide to BEING MORE PRODUCTIVE

Early risers are often more successful than those who sleep in. This is because they have more time to get things done. They can also get a head start on their day and avoid the rush of trying to do everything at the last minute.

If you want to be more productive, try setting your alarm clock for an earlier time and see how it affects your productivity. Being able to make the most of your day by getting up earlier is a given that you will have more time to get things done. That extra time can be a cushion for you when you are under a time crunch.

Productive people use the most of their time and try to squeeze another hour out of a full day.

2. Create A To-Do List

To-do lists should be created daily as a routine habit.

To help you feel like a superhero and ultimately finish off your to-do list, I propose that you choose three objectives for each day so that you can achieve them. Remember to give importance to the items on the list and check them often. I prefer to start with the essential activities, especially those that would take up the most of my time.

You'll discover that you have much more time in the afternoon when you work from the most difficult to the most straightforward activity. Checking things off as completed can also help you feel good about yourself and motivated.

3. Use Sticky Notes

Some of us utilize our phones to remind us of things. However, if your phone dies or you accidentally hit the snooze button, you might miss an important reminder! Sticky Notes ensures you don't forget anything on your to-do list, whereas Sticky Note can help you remember everything.

Kailin Gow's Go Girl Guide to BEING MORE PRODUCTIVE

Sticky Notes are great for keeping track of appointments, quotations, and visualizations. They now come in various hues, sizes, and designs, so it should be a fun and engaging way to get stuff done!

For example, if you have a stack of letters that need to be mailed and are on your to-do list, why not put a sticky note on top of the pile with a deadline for sending them? It will serve as a motivator to get them out of the way. Although it may seem old-fashion, it is still effective.

If you do not have stick it notes to remind yourself to do your tasks, you can use the digital version which is an app on your phone. Scheduling to do tasks on your phone is the to-do list of today and can keep you organized and on top of everything, especially when you have many tasks to do.

4. Record It

Of course, you may take notes digitally using note-taking applications or a text document, but have you considered recording them on a digital recorder?

If writing things down is too much of a bother, this is a quick and straightforward approach to getting things done.

You may download free recording applications for your smartphone. You may replay the recording and listen to your ideas by making a voice recording. This will allow you to hear things from a different perspective.

5. Create A Schedule

If you want to be more productive, it is essential that you create a schedule and stick to it.

A schedule will help you use your time wisely and avoid wasted time. It can also help you stay on track when working on multiple tasks.

Kailin Gow's Go Girl Guide to BEING MORE PRODUCTIVE

Creating a schedule is simple. Start by listing all the tasks you need to complete in a day. Then, assign a time for each task. Be realistic when creating your schedule and allow yourself some flexibility.

Once you have created your schedule, stick to it as much as possible. This will help increase your productivity and help you get more done in less time.

As stated earlier, you can use your phone or computer to digitally schedule your tasks and events so that you will be reminded of and alerted to upcoming tasks and events that will keep you on schedule and organized.

6. Use Pen And Paper

In an increasingly digitized world, it can be easy to forget the power of pen and paper.

Writing things down on paper can help you organize your thoughts and ideas. It can also help you remember things better than if you were to type them out on a computer.

If you want to be more productive, try taking notes by hand instead of on a laptop or tablet. You may be surprised at how much more effective it is.

7. Prioritize

Take some time to be realistic. Not all activities and occurrences are created equal, and you can't do everything! Find a means to draw attention to critical events so you can see them immediately and guarantee you don't miss them.

On your to-do lists, always put these items at the top and get them out of the way first. Consider moving unimportant or non-time-critical tasks off your current list and onto another day if there are any.

8. Delegate

You cannot do everything by yourself, and that is okay!

Kailin Gow's Go Girl Guide to BEING MORE PRODUCTIVE

To be more productive, you need to learn to delegate tasks. This will allow you to focus on the most important things and get them done more quickly.

Start by identifying the tasks that you can delegate. Then, find someone willing and able to help you with those tasks. This could be a friend, family member, or co-worker. Once you have delegated the task, follow up and ensure it has been completed. This will help you stay on track and be more productive.

Implications of Poor Time Management

Did you know that poor time management ripple effects nearly every aspect of your life? When you don't manage your time well, it can lead to:

1. Poor workflow

Your productivity suffers when you can't plan ahead and stick to objectives. For instance, if there are several vital activities to complete, a good strategy would be to accomplish them in sequence or consecutively. However, if you don't plan ahead, you might have to repeat steps or retrace your steps while doing your job. That translates into lower efficiency and productivity.

2. Wasted time

Poor time management might result in lost time. For example, while completing an assignment, chatting with friends on social media distracts you and consumes time that could be used for other tasks. This can lead to procrastination and, as a result, decreased productivity.

3. Loss of control

If you can't manage your time, it's easy to feel like you're not in control of your life. This can lead to anxiety and stress, which are major productivity killers. So as you can see, bad time management habits can have far-reaching implications. That's why it's essential to develop good habits that will help you be more organized and productive. Read on to learn about some of the top habits of highly productive people.

Kailin Gow's Go Girl Guide to BEING MORE PRODUCTIVE

4. Poor quality of work

When you're rushed, it's harder to produce high-quality work. This is because you don't have enough time to proofread, edit, and revise your work before submitting it. As a result, you might get lower grades or feedback on your work.

5. Poor reputation

Expectations and opinions are harmed if you cannot complete tasks on time for clients or your employer. If a customer can't count on you to deliver something on time, they'll look for alternatives. This can lead to a loss of business or opportunities.

The Benefits Of Time Management

You may be asking, "How can I make myself more productive?" It helps to have a solid motivation – to understand why it's worth the effort to pursue time management practices.

Kailin Gow

What's the purpose of mastering time management? To be successful. And it's not only about work success. Time management abilities are required for all forms of success, from being an excellent friend to becoming a fantastic parent to achieving excellence in your health.

It's impossible to achieve anything significant in any area without putting in the effort. Time is one of the essential things you have. Learning how to manage your time is an excellent use of your time because it gives you more time to do the things you want and needs to do.

Many benefits come with being a master of time management. These benefits include:

Less stress: Poor time management can lead to much stress. If you feel like you're constantly running behind or forgetting things, that's a sign that your time management skills could use some improvement.

More free time: Once you get a handle on your time, you'll be surprised at how much free time you have.

Kailin Gow's Go Girl Guide to BEING MORE PRODUCTIVE

And with that extra free time, you can finally start pursuing your hobbies or spending more time with loved ones.

Better work/life balance: If you can get your work done efficiently, you'll have more time for your personal life and hobbies. This is important for maintaining a healthy lifestyle and avoiding burnout.

Increased productivity: Time management leads to increased productivity because it allows you to focus on one task at a time and eliminates distractions.

Improved decision making: When you're organized and clearly understand what needs to be done, you can make better decisions.

There are many helpful ways to be more organized and productive in your everyday life. By incorporating some of the top habits of highly effective people, you can supercharge your productivity and get more done in less time. So, start implementing these habits today and see how much more productive you can be!

Chapter Four

Overcoming Procrastination

It's Friday afternoon, and the deadline is rapidly approaching. You're working as fast as possible to finish a project before 5 p.m., but you're also silently blaming yourself for not having begun sooner.

What caused this? What went wrong? Why did you lose your concentration in the first place?

There were the hours you spent re-reading emails and checking social media, the "excessive preparation," coffee breaks, and the time wasted on activities you could have postponed until next week.

You can probably relate to this feeling of lost productivity. We've all been there at some point or another. Maybe you're in the midst of it right now. But what if I told you that there's a way out? That by making some simple changes to your habits, you can overcome procrastination and become more productive?

Procrastination is a trap that many of us fall into. It's easy to do and hard to break out of. But you can dramatically impact your productivity by understanding the causes of procrastination and implementing some proven strategies.

Is Procrastination the Same as Being Lazy?

Procrastination and laziness are frequently conflated, but they are not the same.

Procrastination is a deliberate behaviour that involves deciding to do something other than the chore you know you should be performing. In contrast,

Kailin Gow's Go Girl Guide to BEING MORE PRODUCTIVE

procrastination implies passivity, inactivity, and an unwillingness to take action.

Procrastination generally entails putting off an unpleasant yet more important task in favor of something more pleasurable or less difficult.

However, succumbing to this urge might have dire consequences. Even little bouts of procrastination may make us feel guilty or ashamed. It can cause a drop in productivity and fail to meet our objectives.

If we put off working for a long time, we may become demotivated and dejected about our career, which can lead to sadness and even job loss in severe situations.

On the other hand, laziness is an unwillingness to work or exert oneself. It's more about apathy and a lack of motivation than anything else.

Lazy people don't want to put in the effort required to achieve their goals. They would instead do nothing or just the bare minimum rather than put forth the time and energy needed to succeed.

While laziness may lead to procrastination, the two are not the same. You can be lazy and not procrastinate (i.e., you might not care about your work but still do it on time), or you can procrastinate without being lazy (i.e., you might care about your work but still find yourself putting it off).

The method in Overcoming Procrastination

It's possible to break free from procrastination like any other habit. Follow these guidelines to assist you in coping with and preventing procrastination:

Step 1: Recognize That You're Procrastinating

The first step is acknowledging that you have a problem with procrastination. This may seem obvious, but it's essential, to be honest with yourself before making any real progress.

You may be putting off something because you've had to re-prioritize your tasks. If you're delaying an essential activity for a genuine reason, you aren't necessarily procrastinating. However, if you're putting off a task because you don't want to do it or because you're afraid of failing, then you are procrastinating.

Step 2: Work Out WHY You're Procrastinating

Before you can begin to address procrastination, you need to know why you're doing it. Are you avoiding something because it's unpleasant or monotonous? If this is the case, take action to get rid of it as soon as possible so that you can focus on the parts of your job that appeal to you.

Kailin Gow

Procrastination is a result of poor organization. Organized individuals successfully combat this by using prioritized To-Do Lists and establishing efficient schedules. These instruments allow you to categorize your activities according to their importance and deadline.

Even if you're a disciplined person, an activity may overwhelm you. Perhaps you are concerned about your ability and failing, so you put it off and seek comfort in completing tasks you know you can accomplish.

Some individuals are terrified of success, just as they are of failure. They believe that if they succeed, they'll be deluged with requests to complete more assignments.

Perfectionists, surprisingly, are frequently procrastinators. Instead, they'd put off doing a task they believe they lack the abilities to do rather than do it incorrectly and receive criticism.

Kailin Gow's Go Girl Guide to BEING MORE PRODUCTIVE

Step 3: Adopt Anti-Procrastination Strategies

Procrastination is a habit, which means it's difficult to break. This implies that you're unlikely to be able to break your procrastination overnight. Habits only cease being habits when they are avoided; as a result, use any of the techniques below to increase your chances of success.

Forgive yourself for procrastinating in the past: Self-forgiveness has been shown to improve feelings of self-esteem and decrease the chance of procrastination in the future.

Start with baby steps: Set small, achievable goals rather than attempting to accomplish too much at once.
Focus on the present moment: Concentrate on what you're doing now and resist the urge to think about other tasks you need to complete.

Change your environment: Sometimes, all you need is a change of scenery. If you can't concentrate where you are, try working in a different location.

Set a time limit: Give yourself a specific time to work on a task before taking a break.

Use positive reinforcement: Reward yourself for completing tasks so you'll be more likely to stick with your new habit.
Break up large tasks into smaller ones: This will make them seem less daunting and increase the likelihood that you'll start working on them.

Set deadlines: A looming deadline is often enough to motivate people to start a task.

Find an accountability partner: Tell someone else about your goals and ask them to check in with you regularly to see how you're progressing.

Kailin Gow's Go Girl Guide to BEING MORE PRODUCTIVE

Just get started: The most challenging part of any task is usually getting started. Once you've overcome that initial hurdle, it's much easier to keep going.

Commit to the task: Stop focusing on avoiding and start focusing on doing. Make a list of everything you need to accomplish and the times you'll do them. This will aid in your ability to confront your duties proactively.

Promise yourself a reward: Reward yourself with a treat, such as a slice of cake or a cup of coffee from your favorite cafe, after finishing an arduous activity on time. Make sure you remark how wonderful it feels to complete things!

Ask someone to check up on you: Peer pressure can be helpful! This is the basis for self-help organizations. If you don't have anyone to ask, a website like Procraster may assist with self-monitoring.

Kailin Gow

Procrastination is putting off a necessary activity by focusing on more enjoyable, less urgent, or less important tasks. It's not synonymous with slothfulness, which is the refusal to act.

Procrastination may stifle your potential and destroy your career. It can also upset teamwork, decrease morale, and cause depression and job loss. As a result, it's critical to take preventative action now.

Recognizing that you're procrastinating is the first step to overcoming it. Then, figure out why you're doing it and how you may manage and overcome it using appropriate methods.

Chapter Five

Developing a Positive Attitude

Even if you enjoy your employment, things may go wrong. You may be side-tracked by an irate client, a support issue, or a sense of lethargy in the workplace.

While one bad experience might be easy to fall into a funk, it is just as simple to redirect your attention and focus instead on the — hopefully more — positive experiences.

There are methods for cultivating and maintaining a positive attitude, as well as the most powerful words that can assist you in maintaining a good perspective at work and in life.

A good attitude entails being optimistic about events, interactions, and yourself. People with good attitudes maintain a positive outlook and see the finest in even critical circumstances. On the other hand, those with negative attitudes may be more pessimistic and disagreeable, and they frequently anticipate the worst outcome in challenging situations.

A good attitude does not always mean you are less stressed, but it can provide the tools you need to deal with stress more healthily. Let's look at how a positive attitude may be seen in your work and personal life.

Why is having a positive attitude important?

You can deal with stress and unpleasant circumstances more healthily if you have a positive mental attitude.

You may not be afraid of stress as a physically dangerous thing, but you may fear it as a means to an end. Other advantages include establishing actionable objectives based on aspirations, cultivating more satisfying relationships, and providing your immune system with a much-needed boost.

The following are some of the ways that a positive attitude manifests itself:

You'll be more optimistic.

A more optimistic perspective of life is not only the result of having a good attitude. Instead of believing, "the grass on the other side is greener," you'll believe that you're already on greener pastures. You'll focus on the bright side of most things, allowing you to face challenging situations with optimism.

This perspective is contagious. You'll start to see the good in people and circumstances more frequently, making you a more pleasant person to be around. Additionally, this mindset attracts others who are optimistic as well.

You'll have a better time dealing with letdowns and failures.

You can still be aggressive, but you'll cope and bounce back. Not only that, but you may accept that things happened the way they did rather than remaining in denial. Those with a negative attitude will dwell on unpleasant experiences and often fail to learn from their mistakes. On the other hand, people with a positive outlook will use these experiences as learning opportunities.

You'll be more resilient.

It might not seem like it, but having a good attitude can make you more mentally tough. You'll be able to take on new challenges and put in the extra effort required because you know it's worth it. A negative attitude will only bring you down and make you want to give up when things get tough.

Kailin Gow's Go Girl Guide to BEING MORE PRODUCTIVE

You'll have more incredible physical stamina and energy levels.

Our attitudes determine a lot of what we feel. When we're happy, we tend to have more energy. We also don't get as quickly tired, both physically and mentally. On the other hand, when we're down, everything feels like a drag. To be more productive, it's essential to have the physical and mental energy required.

Productive people prioritize physical activity as a way to lower stress, build strength and stamina, as well as staying healthy. You can easily and seamlessly incorporate physical activity into your life by taking stairs, growing your own food through gardening, doing your own household chores, doing things yourself.

Not only by doing things yourself and growing your own produce, you have more control over the quality of your food, over the way you would want your food cooked, etc. etc. Plus, you will be able to save yourself money, which you can put into other things you enjoy.

You'll be able to handle stress better.

It's not that having a positive attitude will make stress disappear. However, you'll be better equipped to deal with it constructively. You may even find that you don't get as stressed out in the first place because you're not dwelling on negative thoughts.

Creative Ways to Keep a Positive Attitude

Staying positive can be challenging when life gets overwhelming, but it's essential to maintain a good attitude if you want to be productive. Here are some creative ways to keep your spirits up:

1. Start a gratitude journal.

Why not remind yourself of all you have to be grateful for daily? There's so much to be thankful for in life, so why not think about it daily?

Kailin Gow's Go Girl Guide to BEING MORE PRODUCTIVE

A gratitude diary is an excellent method to keep the good vibes going all day. Each day, list at least three things for which you are grateful. They may be as little as seeing a cute puppy on your way to work or as significant as getting a job offer for your ideal position. Furthermore, they might be anything that happened to you on that particular day — such as having a large latte—or anything that exists in your life permanently, like being loved by your family.

You're in control. Whatever you want to write is entirely up to you. All that matters is that you remember to be grateful every day. You can improve your attitude by retraining your thoughts to consider all the beautiful things in your life.

2. Treat yourself to some self-care every day.

It's critical to maintain both your physical and mental health. It may feel overwhelming when you're working a full-time job that requires frequent contact with people — clients, prospects, co-workers, or bosses — in high-pressure situations.

Taking a step back and pampering yourself with something unique is essential to keep moving forward with a good attitude. Self-care does not have to be limited to soaking in the bath with candles and a glass of wine, although that is certainly nice.

Consider how you may unwind, de-stress, and reclaim some "you" time. Face masks, movies, baking, reading, calling a friend, taking out delivery, or even just saying "no" to plans and staying in are good options. Make it a habit to do something every day. By allowing yourself these relaxation times, you can cultivate a more optimistic attitude while working hard.

3. Start every morning strong.

It's simpler to sustain a good mood all day if you start it right after waking up. The sound of the alarm may frequently lead to annoyance, which sets you on the road to having an overall negative attitude.

Try to avoid that by getting up immediately instead of hitting the snooze button. Make your bed as soon as you get out of it, so you have one less thing to do later. Eat a nutritious breakfast and take some time to think about your goals for the day. This will help you center yourself before starting work and prevent little things from derailing your attitude later.

4. Avoid spreading gossip.

Gossiping is a vicious habit that can quickly turn into a negative mindset. It's easy to get caught up in talking about other people's business, but it's important to remember that words have power.

Before speaking, think about how your words might affect the person you're gossiping about and the person you're speaking to. Would you want someone speaking about you in that way? Gossiping only leads to negativity and drama, so it's best to avoid it altogether.

It also takes away from your time and energy which is counter-productive. Negative activities that cause you and others stress such as gossiping not only waste time and energy, but create an overall negative work environment. Want to have more of a lasting effect on your team? Try to focus on ways to boost everyone's productivity with positivity. Here are some ways to be more positive.

5. Crack more jokes.

A little laughter goes a long way. You're more likely to maintain a positive attitude if you find humor in everyday situations. You're less likely to get frazzled by the small stuff when you have a good sense of humor.

And studies show that laughter is good for your health! It boosts your immune system, eases stress, and relaxes your body. So go ahead and crack a few jokes — it might be the key to being more productive.

Kailin Gow's Go Girl Guide to BEING MORE PRODUCTIVE

6. Take real breaks.

Taking breaks throughout the day is essential, but it's just as important to ensure those breaks are meaningful. Instead of scrolling through social media or reading the news, use your break time to do something that will refresh and rejuvenate you.

Go for a walk outside, read a few pages of a book, or meditate for a few minutes. Do some stretches, jog in place, get some fresh air, and/or eat a delicious and healthy snack like an apple, orange, nuts, or berries. Whatever you do, make sure it's something that will help you clear your mind and return to work feeling refreshed and ready to tackle whatever comes your way.

7. Practice meditation.

Meditation can help relieve tension and anxiety and enhance mental and spiritual wellbeing. Meditation may help people in high-pressure jobs, such as customer support or service, reduce workplace anxiety.

Even five minutes per day is a wonderful start to meditation practice. Deep breathing and mental relaxation are essential techniques in this exercise. Simple methods like these, which are simple to implement, will help you achieve peace of mind and release the negativity and tension you encounter daily.

By following these tips, you can develop habits that will help you be more organized and productive. Implementing even a few of these habits into your daily routine can significantly improve your overall productivity. So, start today and see how much more you can get done!

Positive Attitude Examples

It's been said that a positive attitude is a key to success. And it's true! A positive attitude can go a long way in making you more organized and productive. After all, if you believe you can accomplish something, you're

Kailin Gow's Go Girl Guide to BEING MORE PRODUCTIVE

much more likely to do it. Below are some examples of positive attitudes:

1. Looking at the Bright Side After Getting Laid Off

If you've been laid off, you know how awful it is. You feel like your value has been questioned because you weren't valuable enough to stay on the company's payroll. Even if it wasn't by choice but rather owing to financial strain, it might be devastating, especially if you have a family to care for.

It would be easy to let this event spiral into a negative attitude. You might start thinking that you're not good enough, that you'll never find another job, and so on. But if you want to stay productive and organized, it's important to resist these negative thoughts. Instead, try to think of the situation in a more positive light.

For example, you can tell yourself that getting laid off was a blessing in disguise. It's allowed you to spend more time with your family or pursue other interests outside of work. And who knows? Maybe the next job you get will be even better than the last one.

By looking at the bright side of things, you'll maintain a positive attitude and be more likely to stay productive, even in challenging circumstances.

2. Practicing Self-Care after a Failure at Work

It's too easy to feel discouraged after making work mistakes. It's possible that you didn't adequately prepare a presentation, your inefficiency ruined your productivity, or your supervisor had to meet with you again about your performance. Whatever the case, it's important not to dwell on your failures.

Negative thinking will only lead to more stress and anxiety, making it harder for you to be productive. Instead of wallowing in your misery, try to care for yourself mentally and physically. Indulge in a relaxing activity, such as reading or taking a bath. Exercise, keep yourself healthy so you feel good and ready to face any challenges that come your way. Make sure to get enough sleep so you're well-rested and can face the next day with a clear head.

And most importantly, don't be too hard on yourself! We all make mistakes; it's part of being human. As long as you learn from your mistakes and vow to do better next time, there's no reason why you can't be successful.

3. Meditating When Feeling Overwhelmed at Work

This scenario seems to be all too familiar. You have twenty clients to follow up on, a presentation due this week, and a meeting with higher-ups regarding your team's performance. In most cases, nearly anybody would feel overwhelmed in this scenario. Even if the specifics are varied, we've all felt we were in over our heads at some point.

When you're feeling overwhelmed, it's important not to panic. This will only lead to more stress and make it harder for you to focus on what needs to be done. Instead, take a few deep breaths and try to clear your mind. If possible, step away from work for a few minutes and allow yourself to relax. Maybe listen to some calming music or read a short story.

It's also helpful to meditate on the situation. What is causing you to feel overwhelmed? Is it an unrealistic workload? If so, can you delegate some of your tasks to others? Or is it simply that you're not used to being this busy? In either case, once you've identified the source of your stress, it'll be easier to find a way to cope with it.

4. Finding Worthwhile Pastimes While Stuck in Traffic

Kailin Gow's Go Girl Guide to BEING MORE PRODUCTIVE

Rage is rife these days, especially if you reside in a crowded region. Will you become enraged and try to merge lanes to search for the one going faster? Or will you take a deep breath, crank up the radio, and try to enjoy the extra time you have been given?

The latter is always the better option for your mental state and productivity. While it might be challenging to find the silver lining when you're stuck in traffic, it's essential to try. Maybe you can use this time to listen to an interesting podcast or call a friend you haven't talked to in a while.

If you can stay calm while stuck in traffic, your day will likely go more smoothly overall. You won't be as frazzled when you finally arrive at your destination, and you'll be less likely to make mistakes. So, the next time you find yourself sitting in bumper-to-bumper traffic, take a deep breath and try to relax.

Kailin Gow

If you learn to be more organized and productive, you'll find that you can get more done in less time. Following the tips in this article, you can supercharge your productivity and make the most of your time. So, start implementing these habits today and see how much more productive you can be!

CHAPTER SIX

Planning Ahead

Have you ever attempted to achieve a goal or dream without having a strategy in place or on paper? Have you ever done this before? Were you able to achieve any measurable outcomes if you have? Did you feel disoriented at some time, telling yourself things like "I wish I'd thought of that" or "I wish I'd planned it first"?

Many of us act without taking the time to prepare. You're preparing to fail if you don't plan. Many people fail because they don't take the opportunity to think ahead and create a strategy for success. You have no guidepost to show you which roads will lead you from where you are to where you want to be if you don't make a plan.

Planning is an essential component of achieving dreams. You become proactive and anticipate problems or roadblocks that may arise, so you can prepare the actions to avoid them or face them bravely if they do appear.

Despite the advantages of planning, many of us prefer not to do so in our personal or professional life. We either wait until the last minute to plan what we want to accomplish or take action without forethought. Our lack of enthusiasm for planning is due to our belief system. The following are seven reasons why we avoid preparing in advance.

1. MOST PEOPLE ARE REACTIVE RATHER THAN PROACTIVE

We don't plan to do things or achieve objectives until we are instructed to or it is essential. We don't react appropriately; therefore, our reactive plans rarely work. We will have little interest in planning ahead while remaining in reactive mode. If we want to become proactive and take control of our lives, we must start making plans.

Kailin Gow's Go Girl Guide to BEING MORE PRODUCTIVE

Reactive people tend to be more chaotic and less organized than proactive people. If you're constantly reacting to things that come up, you'll never be able to get ahead or plan for anything. Being assertive means being in control of your life and taking action instead of waiting for things to happen to you.

2. MOST PEOPLE ARE ARE NOT ORGANIZED

Those who plan ahead are generally more organized than those who do not. We may like the concept of being organized or even expect others to be organized, but we do not believe in the value of planning because we are unorganized. Our plans may go wrong; when this happens, we lose interest and become even more chaotic. This cycle repeats itself until we hit a snag and become aware of it.

If you're not organized, it will be challenging to plan ahead. You need to have some sort of system in place so that you can keep track of your goals and what you need to do to achieve them. Being organized doesn't mean that everything has to be perfect all the time. It just means having a system to stay on track and be more productive.

3. MOST PEOPLE ARE ARE NOT SELF-DISCIPLINED

When it comes to self-discipline, disciplined people have order in their personal and professional lives. They possess the resolve to follow their beliefs and take appropriate actions based on sound plans. It's tough to be self-disciplined without a well-thought-out strategy. Self-discipline is not only a demanding but also an open attitude that leads you to accomplish anything.

We avoid following through with our plans when we lack self-discipline, which is why preparing in advance is so difficult. We conclude that planning prevents us from getting up to speed as quickly as possible. We forget that doing whatever we want isn't the same as what needs to be done. We can't get where we want to be faster without a strong strategy and self-control if we don't plan and stick to it.

4. MOST PEOPLE PROCRASTINATE

Some people are naturally good planners, while others avoid making plans altogether. Others put off preparing ahead of time. They postpone the process of planning for success because they believe it is premature to plan, they aren't ready, or they may not need a strategy at all. The more we delay, the more difficult it becomes to create successful strategies that will bring us closer to our goals.

Procrastination is a major obstacle to planning ahead. If you're constantly putting things off, you'll never get around to making a plan. You need to be able to take action and not wait until the last minute. Otherwise, you'll never get anything done and always be behind.

5. MOST PEOPLE DON'T KNOW HOW TO PLAN EFFECTIVELY

Planning ahead necessitates understanding. There are instruments for effective planning, but we won't be perfect planners if we don't know how to use them. As a result, a lack of interest in planning ahead stems from a lack of knowledge about how to do it effectively. We need to educate ourselves on the subject to be better prepared.
Many people don't know how to plan effectively because they've never been taught how. To be a better planner, you must learn about different planning techniques and find one that works best.

6. MOST PEOPLE THINK PLANNING IS A WASTE OF TIME!

Typically, we don't do what we don't believe in. We are correct if we think that plans fail and that planning ahead is a waste of time. What we focus on grows. To change our thinking and see planning as an essential step, we must first alter it.

The biggest reason people don't plan is that they think it wastes time. If you believe planning is pointless, then you're not going to bother doing it. But if you change your mindset and see the value in planning, you'll be more likely to do it.

7. MOST PEOPLE ARE NOT PATIENT

Another cause of why some people dislike preparing is that they are too impatient to wait for the plans to come together. We simply want to start the implementation phase without having a plan. This approach to planning leads to preliminary plans, low productivity, and losses.

When it comes to planning, patience is a virtue. You need to be patient to create a comprehensive and effective plan. If you're too impatient to wait, you'll end up with a poorly thought-out plan that won't get you the desired results.

Kailin Gow

We can work on improving our planning skills by understanding these seven reasons why people don't plan ahead. If we can overcome these obstacles, we'll be well on our way to being more organized and productive. Implementing even just a few of the top habits of highly productive people can make a big difference in your level of productivity. So start making changes today and see how much more organized and productive you can be!

Chapter Seven

Reviewing Your Progress

We are frequently oblivious to change. We may be complacent and ignorant of how far we've come or how far we've gotten toward our objectives, which might be disheartening. When we can't see our accomplishments, it's easy to undervalue them.

On the other side, staying in one place when we wish to progress is also simple. We may not realize that we said we would do something a year ago and have only moved a few steps forward. To safeguard against getting too caught up in our routine, we must be vigilant about our development and make this a habit. Why is it so crucial?

Kailin Gow

When we get too comfortable, we risk not challenging ourselves. This can lead to a feeling of boredom and apathy. If we don't have any goals to strive for, then what's the point? We need to keep pushing ourselves forward to continue growing and learning.

One way to stay on top of your progress is to review it regularly. This doesn't mean you should beat yourself up over every little thing you didn't accomplish. Instead, take a step back and look at the big picture. What did you achieve last month? Last year? Where do you want to be in the next month or year?

It can be helpful to set up some sort of system for tracking your progress. This could be as simple as keeping a journal or using a planner to write down your goals. Whatever works for you, make sure that you're consistent with it.

If you're not making as much progress as you'd like, then don't be afraid to adjust your goals. It's better to have achievable goals than ones so far out of reach that they demotivate you.

Whenever you hit a milestone, take the time to celebrate your achievement! Pat yourself on the back and enjoy the sense of accomplishment. This will help keep you motivated and inspired to continue working toward your goal.

It helps us stay on track.

We all have hectic schedules. There is the business to attend to, family commitments, interests, and plenty of series to watch. It's too easy to forget what we're doing or where we intend to go.

If we examine our progress daily, weekly, or monthly, we can keep our objectives fresh in our minds and ensure we don't get sidetracked by other activities. This will help us stay focused and on track.

Moreover, by monitoring our progress, we can ensure that we make the most efficient use of our time. We can identify areas where we may be wasting time and adjust accordingly.

It's essential to be flexible with your system for tracking progress. What works for you today might not work tomorrow. The most important thing is to find a method that helps you stay organized and productive.

So don't wait any longer; start reviewing your progress today! You'll be amazed at how much more organized and productive you become in no time.

Appreciate your achievements

Taking stock of your progress can assist you in recognizing what you've accomplished. It's too easy to forget something after we've acquired it, which might be disheartening.

Kailin Gow's Go Girl Guide to BEING MORE PRODUCTIVE

When we compare our progress to what we've done, it's more apparent, and we're better able to see how much we've improved and advanced. This, in turn, can give us a much-needed confidence boost and keep us motivated.

Additionally, it's essential to celebrate your successes along the way! Recognizing your achievements will help you maintain perspective and keep going even when things get tough.

Adjust course

In some cases, we may be following the incorrect plan or method. We should not expect to stick with a diet for a year and then discover it was ineffective. It's a waste of time and resources. Tracing our progress allows us to see what works and what doesn't, allowing us to make adjustments as needed.

Let's assume we're in school and preparing for a really crucial exam. We must check our understanding and abilities regularly and test ourselves to ensure that we comprehend everything correctly and employ the best study methods.

The sooner we identify faults or problems, the sooner we can repair them and reach our ultimate objective. Identifying the stumbling blocks in your path is easier when you track your progress. It is simple enough to ignore a few days without working out, but if you keep track of your weekly progress, you'll notice this pattern. It allows you to look at what's going on and figure out what's particularly difficult or gets in your way all the time.

Get motivated by achieving smaller goals.

It can be challenging to stay motivated when we have an important goal. This is because the timeline for achieving the dream may be pretty long, and it's easy to get discouraged when we don't see results immediately.

Kailin Gow's Go Girl Guide to BEING MORE PRODUCTIVE

One way to stay motivated is by breaking down the larger goal into smaller goals. By accomplishing these smaller goals, we inch closer to our ultimate objective and feel a sense of achievement along the way.

This will help us maintain our focus and momentum to continue working toward our larger goal until we reach it.

Share with others

It makes it easier to share your progress with others, whether educating them, assisting them, or getting help for your objectives. It keeps a record of everything you've accomplished without relying on our terrible memories.

It's beneficial for others and can also be a method for you to reflect on what occurred years later. You can see how much you've grown and progressed, which is immensely satisfying.

Additionally, sharing your progress can help hold you accountable. If you know someone is checking in on your progress regularly, you'll be more likely to stay on track and not fall behind.

So don't be afraid to share your progress with others! It can be a helpful tool for staying organized and productive.

More efficient growth

Tracking your progress allows you to see how much effort and time you've put in and the results you've achieved. This is essential knowledge since it will enable you to concentrate your efforts on the most prosperous areas.

You can improve and perfect your process by monitoring what you've done and utilizing that knowledge to grow more efficiently.

Kailin Gow's Go Girl Guide to BEING MORE PRODUCTIVE

Additionally, by understanding what works and what doesn't work, you can avoid making the same mistakes again in the future.

So, there you have it! These are just some of the top habits of highly productive people. By incorporating these habits into your own life, you can supercharge your productivity and get more done in less time. So, start implementing these habits today and see how much more productive you can be!

Chapter Eight: BONUS

100X Your Productivity

What if you can clone yourself so you can get twice as much done?

Today, you can almost do that with technological advances. How?

Find and Sign Up for Apps and Services that will save you time:

1) Online shopping for groceries at stores that will pick out your groceries and deliver them for free or if you purchase a certain limit, will be free. This service saves you time so you won't have to take the time to drive out to the store to pick out groceries.

2) Save time in banking by banking online.

Kailin Gow's Go Girl Guide to BEING MORE PRODUCTIVE

Choose products that do double-duty:

1) Buy products you use often in bulk so you don't have to keep shopping for them. If there is a way to subscribe to a timed delivery of those products, schedule them in so they are automatically delivered. However, with all subscriptions, keep track of your subscriptions so you don't keep paying for items you no longer need.

2) Choose products that can be for multiple uses. For example, shampoo, conditioner, and body wash hybrids make it easier to travel lighter, takes up less space, and takes less time to find. Another example is face foundation that contains sunscreen. When traveling light, you only need one product to accomplish more things like a face foundation with sunscreen that protects you from the sun as well as provide coverage for your skin. If there are moisturizers included, it is even better. One application does multiple jobs.

Kailin Gow

Make The Most of Your Time by Combining Tasks

1) Make errands and trips count. If you need to make an errand, plan out the route where you can accomplish the most in the shortest distance. For example, if you need to go to the store, plan on dropping off your package at the post office along the route, or other stops along the way.

2) Need to post some content for your business? Film a snippet of what you are doing anyways that may be of interest to others. For example, you are baking a birthday cake for a friend, you can film yourself baking, create a story around it, and tie it into a promotional story for your business.

Hire people to take care of the tasks you don't want to do, aren't as good in, or don't have the time to do:

1) This may seem like a no-brainer, but you can save yourself a lot of time and expense if you can find someone who can take care of the tasks you are not good in, don't want to do, or don't have the time to

Kailin Gow's Go Girl Guide to BEING MORE PRODUCTIVE

do so the task gets done faster. This frees up time for you to focus on the work you can do more easily and faster.

2) Take the time to hire good people who will do a great job and won't waste your time. Good people who are competent at their jobs will save you time and frustrations so you should take the time to hire the right person.

Chapter Nine: BONUS

Tools to Become More Productive

As promised, I wanted to include a list of tools that can help you become more productive.

Work and Project Productivity:

1) ToDoist

   A simple task manager app that helps you organize your to do list. Also helps you collaborate with other people.

2) Monday.com

   A project management tool that helps you keep track of workflow as well as expenses.

3) Wrike

Kailin Gow's Go Girl Guide to BEING MORE PRODUCTIVE

A project management tool that helps you plan projects, has time management built-in, and uses advance analytics.

4) Smartsheet

It is a project management software that helps with strategic planning, content management, resource management, and workflow management.

5) Trello

Goal setting, task management, resource management, project management.

6) Adobe Workfront

Budget management, resource management, task management, project management, and demand management.

Household Productivity:

1) Sortly App

    It is an app that helps you sort and organize anything in your house, closet, pantry, etc. simply by taking a photo and then putting it into a folder. You can tag items for easy searching. If you have items in a box for moving or storage, it helps give you an inventory of what's inside your boxes. Best of all, you can include purchase and warranty dates to keep you up to date.

2) Tody App

    It organizes and reminds you when chores like cleaning needs to be done. Family members can track chores and mark them as done, simplifying household chores.

3) Homey

    Another app that helps organize and track household chores, especially with children. When a child finishes a chore, they can mark it off, and allowance payment can be directly paid to them. It teaches them work ethics and financial responsibility.

4) Centriq

   This helpful app removes the clutter of product manuals by simply entering the products you have. Whenever you need to look up their product manual, you can pull it up from the app.

5) Closet+

   YoYoganizes your clothes and accessories in your closet by taking a photo of your clothes and accessories.

Overall Productivity:

1) Google Calendar

   Free calendar that integrates with Google products.

2) MSD Organizer

   Good for organizing budgets.

3) LeaderTask

   Good for organizing team members' time.

4) RoboShark Get Things Done Planner

   Cute paperback project planner for kids and students to help them plan and keep track of projects at school and personal activities

   https://www.amazon.com/Things-Done-Projects-Planner-RoboShark/dp/B0BW2XKH6X

Kailin Gow's Go Girl Guide to BEING MORE PRODUCTIVE

Conclusion

Habits are essential when it comes to being productive. By developing and sticking to good habits, you can supercharge your productivity and get more done in less time. So, if you're looking to boost your productivity, incorporate some of the practices of highly productive people into your daily routine. You'll be surprised at how much more organized and effective you can be!

Following this book's tips and tricks, you can start becoming more organized and productive today. Implement these habits into your daily routine and see how much of a difference they make. You may be surprised at how much more you can get done when you're more organized and productive. So, what are you waiting for? Start becoming a productivity machine today!

Kailin Gow's Go Girl Guide to BEING MORE PRODUCTIVE

About the Author

Kailin Gow is the an award-winning USA Today bestselling author of over 700 books, tv host, award-winning filmmaker, mom, and humanitarian. She lives in California, Las Vegas, and is always on the go! She hosts the Kailin Gow's Go Girl Show and Channel found on Roku, Amazon, and YouTube.

Want to Know More about *Kailin Gow's Books*, Author Insight, Author Appearance, Contests and Giveaways?

Sign Up for Kailin's Free Newsletter at:

Kailin Gow's Go Girl Newsletter

Kailin Gow

Other Kailin Gow's Go Girl Guides!

Kailin Gow's Go Girl Guide to Superfoods (Kailin Gow's Go Girl Guides Series Book 1)

https://www.amazon.com/Kailin-Gows-Guide-Superfoods-Guides-ebook/dp/B0BS6GM7RL

Kailin Gow's Go Girl Guide to The Perfect Cup: TEA Guide (Kailin Gow's Go Girl Guides Series Book 2)

https://www.amazon.com/Kailin-Gows-Girl-Guide-Perfect-ebook/dp/B0BS6GQQ8M

Kailin Gow's Go Girl Guide to BEING MORE PRODUCTIVE

Kailin Gow's Go Girl Guide to The Perfect Cup: Coffee Guide

Coming July 2023!

Kailin Gow's Go Girl Guide to The Perfect Cup: Healthy Smoothies and Juices Guide

Coming July 2023!

Kailin Gow's Go Girl Guide to Travel

Coming July 2023!

Kailin Gow

www.ingramcontent.com/pod-product-compliance
Lightning Source LLC
Chambersburg PA
CBHW020447220526
45464CB00002B/889